Vision of Beauty

The Story of
Sarah Breedlove Walker

Vision of Beauty

The Story of
Sarah Breedlove Walker

KATHRYN LASKY

illustrated by

NNEKA BENNETT

CANDLEWICK PRESS
CAMBRIDGE, MASSACHUSETTS

First paperback edition 2003

The Library of Congress has cataloged the hardcover edition as follows:

Lasky, Kathryn
Vision of beauty: the story of Sarah Breedlove Walker / Kathryn Lasky ;
illustrated by Nneka Bennett.
p.   cm.
Summary: A biography of Sarah Breedlove Walker, who, though
born in poverty, pioneered in hair and beauty care products for
black women, and became a great financial success.
ISBN 0-7636-0253-1 (hardcover)
1. Walker, C. J., Madam, 1867–1919—Juvenile literature.
2. African American women executives—Biography—Juvenile literature.
3. Cosmetics industry—United States—History—Juvenile literature.
[1. Walker, C. J., Madam, 1867–1919. 2. Businesspeople.
3. African Americans—Biography. 4. Women—Biography. 5. Cosmetics
industry—History.] I. Bennett, Nneka, ill. II. Title.
HD9970.5.C672W3547   2000
338.7'66855'092
[B]—dc21   99-19594
ISBN 0-7636-1834-9 (paperback)

2 4 6 8 10 9 7 5 3

Printed in Hong Kong

This book was typeset in Columbus.
The illustrations were done in pencil and watercolor.

Candlewick Press
2067 Massachusetts Avenue
Cambridge, Massachusetts 02140

visit us at www.candlewick.com

Author's Note

'When I was a little girl growing up in Indianapolis, I loved having a lemonade stand. One of my very early memories is coming into the kitchen with a jar full of money and my mother exclaiming, "Goodness, Kathryn, maybe you'll grow up to be the next Madam Walker!"

Madam C. J. Walker became a hero in Indianapolis, Indiana, offering women and girls of all races and classes a powerful role model. She represented a woman's ability to achieve economic power and independence. This book began with my childhood fascination with Madam Walker.

In my research, I discovered many facts about Madam Walker, but there were also gaps in her story. As an author I have tried to fill these gaps by responsibly imagining what she might have felt or wanted. I have not put words in her mouth; all material quoted was actually said by Madam Walker. Also, I decided to use the word "colored" in this book so that my language would be consistent with the era in which Madam Walker lived.

I would like to thank A'Lelia Perry Bundles, Madam Walker's great-great-granddaughter, for the time she spent with me and for the help and information she so generously provided. I was delighted to discover that Ms. Bundles and I had grown up eight blocks from each other in the suburbs of Indianapolis and had ridden our bicycles in the same park.

K.L.

THEY DIDN'T TALK MUCH IN THE MORNING—the woman and the two young girls. Never did. It was too cold. Too cold and dark.

Little Sarah could see her breath making fog in the small cabin. For the first few bone-chilling moments, Sarah tried to stick close to her mother, but she was already bustling about, chopping vegetables for that night's supper. Meanwhile Sarah's older sister, Louvenia, was frying slabs of salt pork, and Sarah had to start the corn-bread batter for breakfast.

When her father and her brother, Alex, got up, the talk started. Just a few words—who'd be working where in the fields that day. If it was plowing time, something about the plow and a repair. If it was picking time, something about the bollworms.

The Breedloves were free now. Slavery had ended in 1865, and Sarah, born December 23, 1867, was the youngest and first free-born child of Minerva and Owen Breedlove of Delta, Louisiana, a small town near the Mississippi River.

The Breedloves were sharecroppers and lived and worked on their former master's cotton plantation. They had to buy supplies from him and rent his equipment to tend their crops. Then they had to sell the crops back to him at the prices he set. It was almost like slavery because they usually owed more than they had earned. But the Breedloves were free, and if you were free you could dream.

Owen and Minerva Breedlove dreamed of educating their children. So when they did not talk about plow repairs and cotton, they talked about books and learning to read. Alex, Louvenia, and Sarah were sent to school, but school was open only for the few months between the cotton harvest and planting season. And schoolhouses for colored children were often burned down by white hate groups like the Ku Klux Klan and the White Brotherhood.

The Klan was especially terrifying. The men in the Klan called themselves knights and rode through the southern countryside wearing white hoods and carrying flaming torches. Sarah and her sister and brother had seen schoolhouses burning at night, and the next morning they had walked through the ruins. The Klan believed that an educated colored person was dangerous. If colored people could read and write, there was no telling what they might do.

DELTA, LOUISIANA
MID 1870s

THE SUN WAS JUST COPPERING THE COTTON fields when the Breedloves got there each morning. Sarah had worked in the fields since she was five years old, first carrying water, then planting seeds in the freshly turned earth. By the time she was ten she would be old enough to push a plow.

After twelve hours in the cotton fields, Sarah returned home with her family and began digging potatoes for the next night's supper. Then she fed the chickens and swept the yard. On Saturdays, Minerva Breedlove and the two girls washed their own clothes and those of white people. For this they were paid one dollar a week.

Most of the time it was blistering hot. In the fields, Sarah and her mother and sister kept their heads tightly wrapped in bandannas, or "do rags," to soak up the sweat and protect their hair from the sun.

On Sundays, they unwrapped their heads from their do rags and went to church. If Minerva Breedlove had time and wanted her girls to look

especially nice, she would divide their hair into sections, twist each one tightly, and tie it with string. Their scalps felt so tight that Sarah and Louvenia could hardly blink or smile. When the hair was combed out, it was straighter, less nappy and knotty, which made Sarah almost forget the pain.

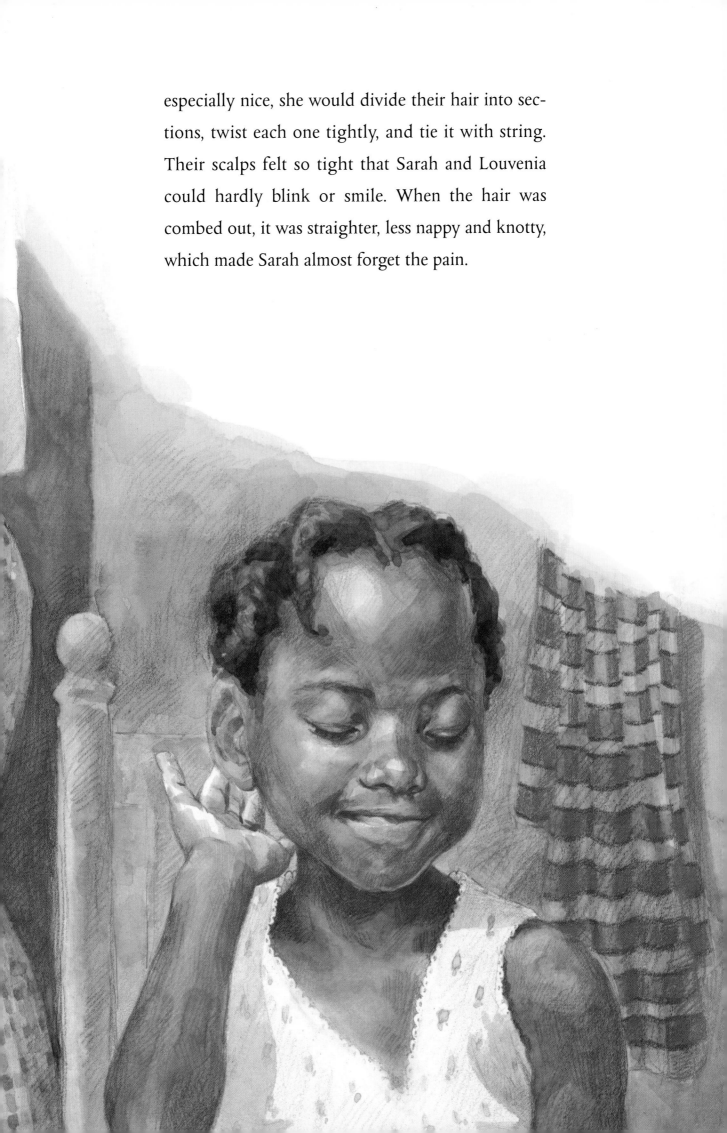

DELTA, LOUISIANA–VICKSBURG, MISSISSIPPI
1875–1882

YELLOW FEVER, CONSUMPTION, AND CHOLERA were constant threats in the hot, humid, low-lying towns near the Mississippi River. Weakened by poverty and hard labor, Owen and Minerva Breedlove could not easily fight such diseases. By 1875, Sarah, Louvenia, and Alex were orphaned. Sarah was only seven years old. She missed her parents desperately and she missed their dreams. Alex soon moved to Vicksburg, a bigger town across the river, to look for work. Sarah and Louvenia had to do laundry day and night. It was the only way they could survive.

The girls were lucky to escape these diseases, but many of the white people who paid them to do laundry died. Then the crops failed in the Mississippi delta. There was no way for the girls to make money.

To escape their troubles, Sarah and Louvenia would walk down to the river and watch the passengers getting off the ferry from Vicksburg. Sarah loved to see the women travelers. Their thick hair pouffed

out like glossy blossoms from under beautiful big hats. She could almost hear the swish of the fancy dresses, but something more than the women's clothes caught Sarah's eye—it was their proud looks, the confident way they held their heads and carried themselves.

At last the girls decided to cross the river to Vicksburg themselves, where they heard there was more work. They took the same boat the grand ladies took, except that Sarah and Louvenia were painfully thin and dressed in rags.

Many white people believed that the end of slavery had brought hard times. They blamed their misfortunes on free colored people. During the 1880s, there were frequent mob killings, or lynchings, of colored people by the hooded knights of the Ku Klux Klan and other white hate groups. Helpless and frightened, colored people began to dream of escaping the South.

Soon after Sarah and Louvenia got to Vicksburg, a traveling preacher began to spread the word that a ship would come to carry colored people to freedom and safety in Africa. Crowds of people waited by the river, dreaming of deliverance, but the ship never came.

Sarah's life was almost worse than it had been in Delta. Louvenia had married a cruel, dangerous man, and the three were crowded together in a small shack. When Sarah could stand it no longer, she married a Vicksburg laborer named Moses McWilliams to get away. She was fourteen years old.

ST. LOUIS, MISSOURI
LATE 1880s

SARAH CALLED OUT TO HER DAUGHTER, Lelia, not to run out of the yard. Sweat was streaming from her bandanna. Her back ached as she turned and plunged her hands into the washtub again. Sarah was not yet twenty, but she was already a mother and a widow. Moses McWilliams had been a good man, but he died before Lelia turned three.

Sarah had moved to St. Louis, where she had heard laundresses could earn good money. St. Louis was a flashy town, full of noise and ragtime music, saloons and dance halls, gamblers and musicians, hustlers and hardworking folks. And it had one of the country's largest colored communities.

Every night when Sarah finished her work, she would take off her bandanna and find broken strands of hair. Years of poor nutrition and hard labor had left her hair brittle and unhealthy—and now Sarah was going bald. She had tried many of the so-called cures and products guaranteed to

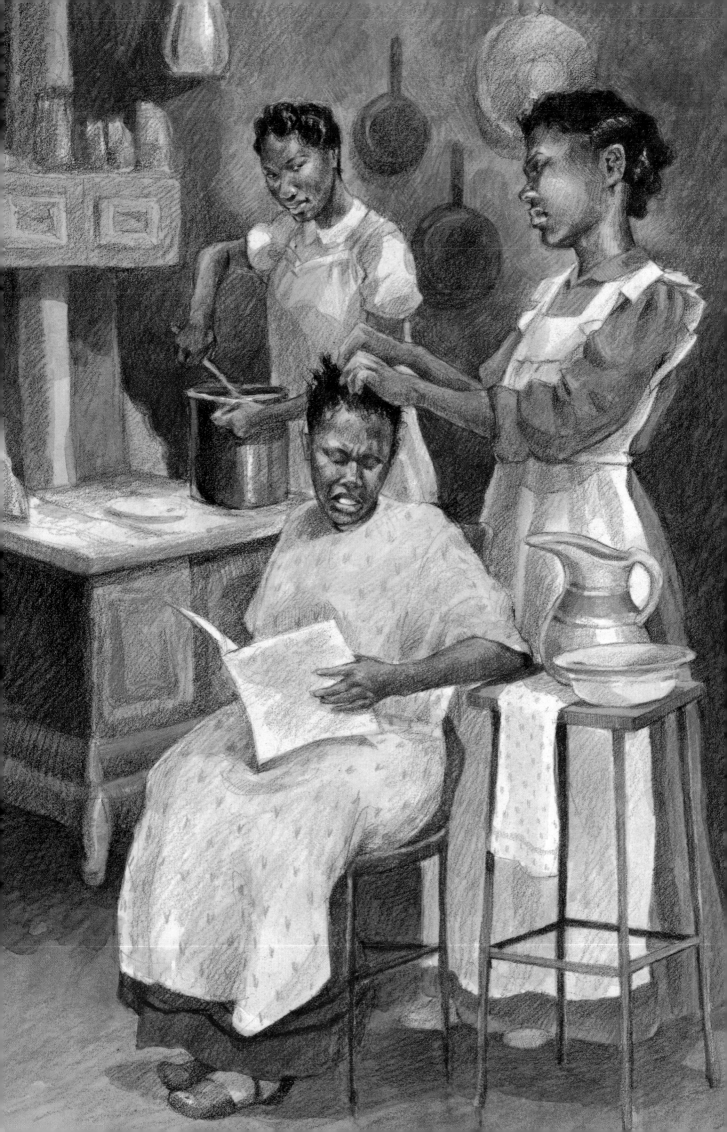

make hair grow — La Creole Hair Restorer, Queen Pomade, Kinkilla. But none worked. Many made her hair worse.

Sarah had spent time in women's kitchens as they tried to straighten and restore their hair. The air was filled with the smells of hot grease, melting wax, and harsh chemicals as the women's hair was fried and their scalps were burned.

Several evenings a week, Sarah put on her best dress and collected money for St. Paul's African Methodist Episcopal Church. The church meant a great deal to Sarah. Before the Civil War, when it was illegal for colored people to go to school, the church had defied the law and taught them to read and write.

Although she was only a poor laundress, each week Sarah put aside a small part of her wages. She was determined to give her daughter the education she had dreamed of for herself. By 1902, Sarah had saved enough money to send Lelia to Knoxville College, a small colored school in Tennessee.

ST. LOUIS, MISSOURI
1904

THE 1904 ST. LOUIS WORLD'S FAIR LASTED the whole year, filling the city with excitement. Famous people were there—famous white folks, and famous colored folks like the poet Paul Laurence Dunbar, the scholar W.E.B. Du Bois, the newspaper tycoon T. Thomas Fortune, and the educator Booker T. Washington.

Sarah was present the night that Margaret Washington, wife of Booker T., addressed the St. Louis chapter of the National Association of Colored Women (NACW). She spoke of the development of colored women, reminding her audience of the NACW's motto, "Lifting as we climb."

Not only was Margaret Washington well-spoken, she was immaculately dressed. Her posture was proud and erect; her hair was thick and healthy. Mrs. Washington seemed like those grand ladies coming off the ferryboat in Delta so long ago. She had their confidence, their independence. That was what Sarah wanted. But how to achieve it?

That night, when Sarah returned home, she got down on her knees and she prayed to God. She prayed for one very simple thing: that her hair not fall out anymore.

The next morning there was still hair on Sarah's pillow but she did not despair. She knew what to do. For that night she had had a dream—a dream of Africa. In it she saw the earth, the soil, the vast grassy savannahs. She saw the plants, the trees, the flowers, the leaves. And she imagined the natural oils and other ingredients that were produced by this vegetation—ingredients that she could use on her hair.

Sarah got busy right away. She began searching out the ingredients and discovering what herbs and oils were to be found in the United States. Some of the ingredients, like tetter salve and sulfur petrolatum, she sent away for; others she was able to purchase in local pharmacies.

DENVER, COLORADO
1905–1908

'WHEN SARAH LEARNED THAT HER BROTHER, Alex, had died, she moved to Denver to be near his wife and children. She rented an attic room there and set up a makeshift laboratory, surrounding herself with pots and glass beakers filled with mixtures. Sarah adjusted and refined and remixed to get the formulas just right, making careful notes in her wobbly handwriting. She spelled as best she could, but her writing was far from perfect.

Sarah could work on her formulas only at night. During the day she was a cook for Mr. E. L. Scholtz, who owned the largest pharmacy in Denver. Some of the ingredients and chemicals she used were the same as those carried in his pharmacy.

When Sarah made a batch she thought was right, she tried it. Soon her hair started growing in faster than it had ever fallen out. Though the ingredients she used were strong, they did not burn hair; and when they were mixed in the right combination, they healed the scalp and made hair healthy.

Sarah decided to go into business for herself.

Soon, she had three products ready for sale: Vegetable Shampoo, Wonderful Hair Grower, and Glossine. She began going door-to-door, giving demonstrations in colored women's kitchens. First she would wash a woman's hair with the Vegetable Shampoo. Next she would apply the Wonderful Hair Grower to nourish her scalp. And then, with a specially designed metal comb heated on the gas stove, she would press in the Glossine, a light oil that softened the woman's tight curls.

In these kitchens, Sarah never said the words "bad hair," which meant kinky and nappy, or "good hair," which meant straight and glossy. White women had "good hair" and they were held out as models of beauty to colored women with their "bad hair." Sarah thought this was insulting.

Many hair-care companies, especially those owned by white people, advertised to colored women by telling them how unattractive they were. These advertisements glorified long, straight hair, while colored ministers preached against straightened hair and scolded colored women for not remaining as God made them. Sarah believed that such advertising

Mme C. J. Walker's
PREPARATIONS
for the HAIR

Worth more than it Costs

OPEN YOUR OWN SHOP

Secure Prosperity and Freedom

Many women of all ages, confronted with the problem of earning a livelihood, have mastered the

WALKER SYSTEM

ALL Mme. C. J. WALKER'S Inventions are reliable because they restore and beautify the hair without injury to the scalp and are used and endorsed by thousands of Hair Dressers and Scalp Specialists throughout the country, known as the Walker Hair Dressers, having a diploma from the Lelia College of Hair Culture which signifies Mme. C. J. Walker's system.

THERE n o t h i imaginary ab the World-W Fame of M C. J. Walke Ultra-Qual Preparatio None genu without M C. J. Walke seal and sig ture.

Learn
Mme.
C. J.
Walker
System o
Hair Cultu

Lelia College and
Walker Hair Parlor
110 W. 136th St., New York

The culmination of the genius of Mme. C. J. Walker is her wonderful Hair Grower and in itself is a wonderful creation for dandruff and falling hair. In fact, it invigorates dry and lifeless hair and stimulates circulation, thereby causing a new growth.

was misleading and that what a woman did with her hair was a woman's business, not a man's.

Sarah's first advertisements for her new company did not use a light-skinned, straight-haired model. The model Sarah used was herself. Her ads emphasized health—the health of the scalp, and the length of her own healthy hair.

And there was another message too. Some early ads showed two pictures of Sarah side by side. In the "before" picture, her hair is thin and short, and her eyes are cast down shyly. The "after" picture shows Sarah with long, healthy hair, looking directly into the camera. She is bolder and seems to have a clearer sense of self-worth. This message was not lost on colored women.

At that time, women—white and colored—were not permitted to vote or own property. Colored people in many parts of the country had even fewer rights. There were restaurants they could not eat in, separate drinking fountains and restrooms for them, theaters and hotels they could not enter. To be a woman and colored meant that one had almost no position or status.

In 1905, Sarah married Charles Walker, an old friend from St. Louis, and became Mrs. C. J. Walker. However, she chose to call herself Madam C. J. Walker. The word "madam(e)" was often associated with France, considered a worldwide center of fashion, and it conveyed an image of status and dignity.

Sarah decided to name her new company with her new name. It was to be called the Mme. C. J. Walker Manufacturing Company.

PITTSBURGH, PENNSYLVANIA
1908–1911

NOT LONG AFTER MADAM WALKER WAS married, she moved her company to Pittsburgh. There was plenty of steel in Pittsburgh to make the Madam Walker pressing combs and there was a good transportation system for shipping her products. Madam Walker still sold door-to-door, and she and Lelia, who had finished her studies, trained her salespeople, or agents, as she called them, to go into the kitchens of colored women.

All customers were viewed as future agents. The agents who sold Madam Walker products were trained to speak to customers not only about health and beauty but about self-sufficiency as well. They were offering women a vision of freedom and dignity: making money in a respected occupation as a hairdresser or saleswoman while still being good wives and mothers.

When Walker agents visited their customers, they would discuss the benefits of working for the

company—and they would be sure to mention that agents could start out making $5.00 a week. This was an impressive amount. The most a colored woman was likely to make was $2.50 a week; at that time a colored man might make $5.00; a white man could expect to make $17.00 a week.

By 1908, only two years after starting her company, Madam Walker had signed on nearly one hundred representatives. She sold directly to customers in their homes and through the mail. The Mme. C. J. Walker Manufacturing Company was making $400 a week.

That same year in Pittsburgh, Madam Walker and Lelia opened the Lelia College of Hair Culturists. Housekeepers, laundresses, and nursemaids flocked to the college to learn a new profession that would give them pride and financial independence.

A few years later, Madam Walker left Lelia in charge of the business in Pittsburgh and moved to Indianapolis, Indiana, which was closer to the nation's center and major transportation systems. By now the company was making more than $3,000 a week, a sum equal to more than $30,000 a week today. In 1911, for a business run by a colored woman, such earnings were almost inconceivable.

INDIANAPOLIS, INDIANA
1911–1918

MADAM WALKER WORKED HARD, BUT SHE had other interests too. She particularly liked the movies. One evening she took a dime to pay for her ticket and handed it to the woman in the box office of the Isis Movie Theater. The ticket taker pushed the dime back.

"Twenty-five cents," she muttered. "The cost for colored people."

Madam Walker's face froze. She would not waste her breath on the woman. She went directly to F. B. Ransom, her chief lawyer, and instructed him to sue the Isis Theater on the grounds of racial discrimination. Next she hired an architect and began a design for a new building to be called the Walker Building. It would cover an entire city block and, in addition to office and factory space, would include an elegant movie theater especially for the city's colored population. This was the beginning of Madam Walker's contribution to the cultural life of Indianapolis.

Her contribution to the economic life of the community was already well-established. Most of Madam Walker's employees were women from the large colored neighborhood where her headquarters were located. Some of the women were trained as agents and hair culturists; others did clerical work or worked in the Walker factory making, packing, and shipping the products.

Alice Kelly, a former schoolteacher, was one of the first women in America to be a factory supervisor. Because Alice could spell and write better than Madam Walker, she was put in charge of helping her employer learn letter-writing and grammatical skills.

By 1912, there were several hundred people working in the factory in Indianapolis and more than a thousand agents traveling door-to-door. By now Madam Walker ran one of the biggest companies in America.

That year, Madam Walker attended the National Negro Business League convention in Chicago. At this time, she was the richest colored woman in America, and one of the richest colored Americans.

In her elegant clothes, she sat down and listened as Booker T. Washington spoke. She remembered another meeting and one of her original inspirations, Margaret Washington.

Mr. Washington introduced a series of colored men, who described their business successes. Madam Walker repeatedly tried to catch his eye, but he never called on her. Finally, she lost her patience and sprang to her feet. "Surely you are not going to shut the door in my face," she protested. "I feel that I am in a business that is a credit to the womanhood of our race."

A hush fell upon the audience. Mr. Washington looked nervous. The National Negro Business League convention was mostly a conference for successful colored men. Colored women were more commonly home minding the family, cooking, and washing.

"I am a woman who came from the cotton fields of the South. I was promoted from the fields to the washtubs. I promoted myself into the business of manufacturing hair goods. I have built my own factory on my own ground."

As Madam Walker spoke, every person in the room listened. Even if they had not touched a bollworm with their bare fingers, they knew about bollworms, and if they had not seen the hooded Klansmen burn a church or a school, they still could smell the ashes.

"My object in life is not simply to make money for myself, but to use part of what I make in trying to help others," continued Madam Walker. Nobody else at the convention had said that. With these words, Madam Walker proved herself more than equal to any man in that room.

She was not stuck in the cotton fields; she was not stuck at a laundry tub. Through tenacity and faith, Sarah Breedlove Walker had come into her own, bringing thousands of colored women with her and showing countless others the way.

EPILOGUE

The richer Madam Walker became, the more she gave back to the people of her race. She wanted to teach others how to give too. At the Mme. C. J. Walker Manufacturing Company, awards were given for employees who contributed to charities in their communities. "I want to show that Walker agents are doing more than making money for themselves," she explained.

But Madam Walker did live well. She bought herself fancy clothes and cars, and in 1918 she moved into Villa Lewaro, a fabulous mansion she had built in Irvington-on-Hudson, New York, on the Hudson River. Madam Walker knew that because of her wealth and her possessions, people listened to her. She became increasingly bold on the subjects of politics and race.

She marched in the streets of Harlem and she even went to the White House with other distinguished colored citizens to demand a meeting with President Woodrow Wilson to protest violence against colored people. The group was told that the President was too busy to see them; he was occupied with a farm feed bill. Madam Walker exploded in anger: "You are talking to us of animal feed when colored people are being murdered in the streets!"

In April 1919, Madam Walker became seriously ill on a business trip to St. Louis. She sped home in a private railroad car on the 20th Century Limited.

Back at Villa Lewaro, she ordered her accountants to donate $5,000 to the anti-lynching fund of the NAACP (National Association for the Advancement of Colored People); it would be the largest donation the organization had ever received. She was failing fast. Finally, she was so weak she could only whisper the words, "I want to live to help my race." Then Sarah Breedlove Walker closed her eyes and died. She was fifty-one years old.

In the more than seventy-eight years that the Mme. C. J. Walker Manufacturing Company was in business, it always had a woman president, in accordance with Madam Walker's wishes. Although the original company has since been dissolved, it has contributed to the Madam Walker Theatre Center in Indianapolis, which continues her legacy of philanthropy in the African-American community of Indianapolis and beyond.

ILLUSTRATOR'S NOTE

'When I was young, I asked my mother why my hair didn't fly. I wanted it to move when I walked, shook my head, or when the wind blew. But my hair was kinky and puffy, different from the straight hair of the white women I saw on TV, or the bouncy ponytails of the white girls I saw on the street. My mother taught me to love my hair the way it grew naturally, which was easy, because she put it into many styles using braids, cornrows, and Afro-puffs.

I know other black women grew up feeling the same way I first did. Over the years, we've been taught to conform to the standard of beauty set by popular images of white women—and as a result, many black women do not like the natural texture of their hair, thinking it is unattractive and unmanageable. While there are so many beautiful shapes and patterns that black women can use to style their hair, it is still more common to see straight hair styles, which many people see as more beautiful and acceptable.

Madam Walker was a great businesswoman and philanthropist, but she was also a pioneer. She created products that made women's skin beautiful and their hair healthy, and she also catered to the desire of black women to change their natural hair texture—allowing us the freedom to achieve styles common among white women, while also enabling us to recognize and appreciate our own natural beauty.

Whether a woman straightens her hair or not, her beauty radiates from within. Beauty comes in many forms. But personally, I prefer to see women wear their hair in its *healthiest* form—naturally kinky, as I do.

N. B.